The Great Lemonade Standoff

CHARACTERS

Narrator 1

Megan
Vicki's teenage sister

Vicki
an enterprising nine-year-old girl

Narrator 2

Jamal
an enterprising nine-year-old boy

Big Hank
a yard service man

SETTING

A suburban neighborhood

READER'S THEATER

Narrator 1: It is a hot summer day. Vicki is making a sign that says, "Fresh Lemonade, 25 cents" when Megan comes by.

Megan: Going into business, huh?

Vicki: I want to make enough money to buy Mom a birthday present with my own money.

Megan: That will make Mom happy.

Narrator 2: Jamal lives next door to Vicki and Megan. He comes outside just as Vicki is setting up.

Jamal: A lemonade stand? Hmm.

The Great Lemonade Standoff

READER'S THEATER

Vicki: If I sell enough lemonade, I am going to buy my mom a music CD for her birthday. I'll also buy her flowers.

Jamal: Can you make that much money selling lemonade?

Vicki: Big Hank and his yard crew are mowing lawns in the neighborhood today. They'll get hot and thirsty. Plus, there is a big game in the park down the street. Lots of people will walk by here. I will sell lemonade to them, too. I can't wait to add up my money!

READER'S THEATER

Jamal: I could use some extra money. I'm saving for a remote-control car that spins and flips! I bet I could make more money than you.

Vicki: Bet not.

Jamal: Just watch me.

Narrator 1: Jamal goes inside his house and mixes up a pitcher of lemonade to sell. He makes a sign that says, "Even Better Lemonade, 25 cents a glass." He sets up his stand across the street from Vicki's stand.

Vicki: You can't do that. I was selling my lemonade here first.

Jamal: It's a free country.

Vicki: That's not fair. If you sell lemonade here, it will take away my customers.

Jamal: I told you I'd sell more than you. Watch me.

Narrator 2: Jamal sees two people walking to the park.

READER'S THEATER

Jamal: Lemonade! Jamal's fresh lemonade!

Narrator 1: Two people buy from Jamal.

Vicki: This isn't right.

Narrator 2: Vicki looks down the street. She sees two more people walking their way. She quickly crosses out "25 cents" on her sign and writes "20 cents." These people buy lemonade from Vicki.

Vicki: Ha! Now that I'm selling my lemonade for less than yours, I'll get all the customers.

Jamal: Two can play that game.

Narrator 1: Jamal crosses out his price. He writes "15 cents a glass" on his sign. As he is changing his sign, Megan checks up on Vicki, who is crossing out the price on her sign again.

Megan: What's going on?

Vicki: I was selling my lemonade and then Jamal set up a stand. He is getting some of my customers.

Megan: He's selling his lemonade for only 15 cents.

Vicki: I know. So now I'm going to sell my lemonade for 10 cents. I'll get all the customers.

READER'S THEATER

Jamal: Not if I sell my lemonade for 10 cents, too.

Megan: You'll both have to sell a *lot* of lemonade if you're going to make any money!

Vicki: Megan is right. I'll have to sell ten glasses just to make one dollar. I'll never be able to sell that much lemonade with you here.

Jamal: I won't make much money either with you here. I'll never get that car.

Vicki: And I won't be able to buy my mom that present.

Narrator 2: Vicki and Jamal stare at each other. Neither one wants to quit. And both know they can't lower their prices again. Then Big Hank comes by.

Big Hank: Two competing lemonade stands? I'll tell you what. When my men are finished, we'll try both. We'll be thirsty, so make sure you have a lot of lemonade.

READER'S THEATER

Jamal: Now I'm going to make some money!

Vicki: We both will. But even if Big Hank and his men buy all your lemonade, will you have enough money for the remote-control car?

Jamal: Not at 10 cents a glass.

Narrator 1: Vicki and Jamal look at each other.

Vicki: What if . . .

Jamal: . . . we sell our lemonade together?

Vicki: I was just thinking that!

Jamal: We can sell it for 25 cents again. And split the money equally.

The Great Lemonade Standoff

READER'S THEATER

Vicki: I can watch the stand and make more lemonade if we need it. You can go sell lemonade to Hank and his men.

Jamal: Then I'll tell people at the park to come here and buy our lemonade.

Vicki: We'll call it "VJ Lemonade."

Jamal: Great idea, partner.

Narrator 2: Jamal walks down to where Big Hank is planting a tree.

Jamal: Hi, Big Hank. I'm here to take your order for VJ Lemonade.

Big Hank: So you're in business together now? Good idea.

Jamal: How about four glasses?

Big Hank: Okay. And another four glasses when we're done.

Jamal: And another four glasses after that?

Big Hank: What a salesperson! And another four glasses after that.

The End